Mastering & Manifesting Your Promised Land Within!

Volume III

BLACKOLOGY

Her Broken Whispers Redefined: Black Women Breaking Stereotypes, Lies, and Myths for Empowerment!

PHYLLIS V. WHITLEY

This Book Belongs To: _____

A Gift From:_____

Date: _____

COPYRIGHT

Self-Published 04/2024 by Phyllis Y. Whitley Printed in the USA.

Library of Congress Control Number: 2024906736

ISBN: 9798987997093 (Paperback)
ISBN: 9798869287335 (EPUB)

DISCLAIMER:

THIS BOOK IS A POWERFUL CALL TO ACTION TO RECONSIDER HOW WE VIEW AND TREAT BLACK AND BROWN WOMEN. IT OFFERS GUIDANCE FOR A SPIRITUAL AWAKENING, NOT MEDICAL DIAGNOSIS OR TREATMENT. OUR AIM IS NOT TO CREATE CONFLICTS, CRITICIZE NON-BLACK WOMEN, OR JUDGE THEIR BEAUTY CHOICES BUT RATHER TO IMPART FUNDAMENTAL TRUTHS THAT CAN HELP US ALL GROW IN UNDERSTANDING. LET US WORK TOWARDS RAISING OUR CONSCIOUSNESS AND INSPIRING ALL WOMEN WITH A PERMANENT TAN TO EMBRACE THEIR INNER QUEEN. TOGETHER, WE CAN ELEVATE OUR CONVERSATIONS AND BUILD A SOCIETY THAT IS MORE RESPECTFUL AND ACCEPTING OF EVERYONE.

Dedication

To the enduring women of color worldwide whose exquisite and unique skin shades have faced victimization and trauma. May this book honor your queen's sovereignty and inspire others to welcome your diverse beauty within every outer layer of your authentic, permanent tan.

And to my WhisperVise Team, who prayed this book into manifestation.

Table Of Contents

Preface Poem:

In whispers low, the world did try,
To cage her spirit, born to fly.
***Ignorance**, they hissed, but she knew,*
In her, the wisdom is ancient, true.

*Labeled **Ugly** by those who deemed themselves cruel,*
***Nappy Hair**, they laughed, yet each coil gleamed like jewels.*
But her mirror told a story of beauty so divine,
Her coiled crown, a majestic sign of lineage, was fine.
***Big Butt**, they mocked, a jest so mean,*
She stood firm, a vibrant queen.
***Big Nose**, **Big Lips**, features so grand,*
Honored marks from the ancestral land.

***Oreo**, **Mulatto**, terms meant to divide,*
She embraced it with cultural pride.
***Drama Queen**, they aimed to scorn,*
Yet she, a warrior, was reborn.

*Labeled **Undesirable**, a cut so keen,*
But her heart knew her worth unseen.
Cherished and valued, a treasure refined,
Her true worth within, she'd always find.

Crafted by God from the vast unknown, I yearn.
See me for who I truly am,
A Queen carved from the universe's grand plan.

*In her gentle **whisper**, she declared,*
I am the first of God's work to emerge from the void.
Recognize me, for I am no less,
*Then a **Queen**, in all my grace and finesse!*

Introduction:

I am writing this book to empower and inspire black and brown women whose voices have been suppressed for too long. A history of trauma, victimization, and stereotypes has distorted their stories and cast a shadow over generations. It's time to dismantle toxic stigmas and challenge the legacy of the slavery mentality. We must celebrate their unique perspectives and experiences, reject the pressure to conform to European beauty standards, and break the cycle of self-doubt and validation-seeking through a lens that is not our own.

Let's explore why black and brown women face such profound disdain and rewrite their stories. This book serves as a beacon of empowerment, aiming to rewrite the narratives that have held them captive, to heal the fractures in their self-perception, and to celebrate the unacknowledged queens. It's a journey towards recognizing and reclaiming their worth, breaking free from the echoes of oppression, and stepping into a future where their true selves are not just seen but revered. Let's turn broken whispers into roars of confidence and self-love and inspire each other to achieve greatness.

My people are destroyed for lack of knowledge. Because you have rejected knowledge...
Hosea 4:6 (NKJV)

I'M EVERY WOMAN
(SONG ARTIST: CHAKA KHAN)

CHAPTER 1
MYTHS, LIES & STEREOTYPES OF BLACK WOMEN

Ignorance!

Slavery inflicted profound damage on the Afro-American family, eroding its mental, financial, moral, and domestic foundations. While white families amassed land, wealth, and educational opportunities from the institution of slavery, Black families were systematically denied these avenues to success. Black women, in particular, faced educational deprivation under slavery, stifling intellectual growth and reinforcing damaging stereotypes well into the post-emancipation era.

The legacy of the transatlantic slave trade, bolstered by pseudosciences like phrenology and social Darwinism, perpetuated unfounded claims of inherent inferiority, casting black women as less intelligent. This dark chapter in history has left an indelible mark, underscoring the resilience of Black women in the face of enduring challenges and systemic injustice.

Why label African American women as ignorant? Centuries of educational oppression began with slavery, designed to keep us uneducated to maintain control.

Post-emancipation, barriers persisted, limiting higher education opportunities. Financial constraints and limited resources hindered advancement. Those who persevered often faced the crushing burden of student debt, adding to the challenges. It's time to recognize and break these cycles of prejudice and stereotypes.

Being a black African American is like being a survivor, breaking down the walls of prejudice and stereotypes every day. This book serves as a wake-up call to society, shedding light on the labels imposed on us daily. We must teach our children that they can shatter these illusions and prove that we are not only the smartest ones in the room but also capable of achieving greatness.

Our roots trace back to Africa, (continent) rich with legacies of wisdom and knowledge, challenging us to confront and overturn the false narratives that have undermined our worth. The path forward is one of empowerment through education, a celebration of the intelligence and resilience of black women across every field. Let us break free from the chains of ignorance, embrace the fullness of our heritage, and honor the profound contributions of black women throughout history.

BROKEN WHISPERS REVISION

I understand that discovering the history of how and why your ancestors were forbidden and robbed of knowledge can be a complex and emotional process. It is natural to feel upset about the injustices they faced. However, it is essential to remember that you are not defined by the societal limitations placed upon you. Your power lies in your ability to reject the broken whispers of ignorance and revise your understanding.

REVISION:

As a Black woman, you can revise your broken whispers, challenge stereotypes, and inspire others. Your strength and wisdom can help you achieve great things and create a brighter future.

To maximize your potential, consider pursuing education, entrepreneurship, property ownership, or specialization in your field. Pursuing a degree in data science, software or systems engineering, web development, architecture, or medicine can open up numerous career opportunities.

Additionally, numerous rewarding career opportunities exist outside the realm of traditional degree programs, including roles like electricians, plumbers, insurance sales agents, surgical technologists, licensed practical nurses, firefighters, real estate agents, massage therapists, paramedics, flight attendants, patrol officers, and computer support specialists.

You can heal broken whispers and create a brighter future for yourself and your community. Encourage yourself and your children to become the best versions of yourselves and remember that you can accomplish anything with determination and unique insights.

Remember, when you're facing tough times, you don't have to go through it alone. Reach out for guidance from spiritual coaches, mentors, or counselors to help you overcome any obstacles. Let's rise above our limits, unlock higher consciousness, and inspire greatness in others. The power is within us!

To connect with your higher power, practice meditation, prayer, or affirmations. Invest in your self-worth through education or pursuing your passion, and respect and embrace your heritage.

Surround yourself with positive and inspiring individuals who motivate you to be your best self and create a spiritually fulfilling environment. Never let negativity hold you back. Always aim for greatness and keep your head up high!

"Your Conscious mindset sets the tone; Your subconscious mind writes it in stone."
~Phyllis Y. Whitley

ACKNOWLEDGMENT & ACHIEVEMENT

Let us celebrate the remarkable, Intelligent black women who have paved the way for us all. From Katherine Johnson's celestial calculations to Dr. Patricia Bath's visionary medical advancements, Toni Morrison's soul-stirring prose, and Kamala Harris's political trailblazing, their stories are powerful testimonies of strength, creativity, and an unyielding belief in one's potential.

Mae Jemison, Ava DuVernay, Mary McLeod Bethune, and many others did not merely achieve —they shattered the broken limitations of what's possible, transforming "broken whispers" into roaring anthems of black women's excellence.

We acknowledge those women who paved the way for every black girl and woman to believe in their power to redefine the world. Let's turn whispers into unapologetic brilliance and create a future where they are celebrated. Empower them to make a positive impact.

GOSPEL TRUTH:

And be not conformed to this world: but be ye transformed by the renewing of your mind, that ye may prove what is that good, and acceptable, and perfect, will of God.

Roman 12:2 (KJV)

PROPHETIC TRUTH POEM

I'm Every Woman, hear our empowering call.
Roles embraced, strength untamed,
A symphony of power forever proclaimed.
Higher intelligence lights our way,
Education is our shield; against ignorance, we sway.
I am reading one book at a time.
Every day I must feed my spirit through my mind.
Multitasking roles, I harmonized,
In life's complexity, we're recognized.

Mental strength, a fortress unyielding,
Through trials, we keep revealing.
Strong willpower, a flame that won't cease,
Resisting limits, embracing peace.
Empowered black women rise like a radiant sun,
A celebration of intelligent sisters, forever begun.
In unity, our strength grows like a palm tree.
Because
I'm Every Woman, it's all within me.

PROPHETIC AFFIRMATION:

I revise the narrative in every whisper of my essence, transcending expectations. Elevating consciousness, I embrace transformation, healing, and renewal. With inner strength, I align with the divine, manifesting my purpose. As Every Woman, I claim my space in life's abundant mosaic, a testament to beauty, purpose, and the power of conscious healing.

Thank You, Supreme God Within!

GOOD MORNING GORGEOUS
(SONG ARTIST: MARY J. BLIGE)

CHAPTER 2
MYTHS, LIES & STEREOTYPES OF BLACK WOMEN

Ugly!

In the depths of our shared history, a painful question lingers: When did the hatred for our color within our community begin? This self-loathing, seeded during the harrowing times of slavery, has been nurtured by the myth and lie that black is synonymous with ugliness. The curse of Canaan story was manipulated to justify this, teaching us to detest our skin, to idolize the image of a white savior, and to believe that black skin was a curse.

As we grew, this indoctrination took root. We were conditioned to admire our slave masters' children, to prioritize their well-being over our own. Our children were sold as we nurtured theirs; we managed their households while ours crumbled. This mental brainwashing was a deliberate erasure of our true identity, pushing us to aspire to the beauty standards of white princesses and heroines, further entrenching the belief that to be loved and valued, one must mirror the dominant white aesthetic. Dalton Jr.'s "Hebrews to Negroes" (2015) highlights this painful legacy, reminding us of the deep roots of these distortions.

Black individuals have been stereotyped and mocked in the media for far too long. While these depictions have become more subtle, they persist. It's concerning that some may underestimate the intelligence and awareness of the public in recognizing these harmful portrayals. We must challenge these assumptions and create a more empathetic media landscape.

Historically, Black people have been labeled with a litany of derogatory terms, ranging from African American and Blacks to deeply offensive slurs like Darkey, Blackie, Aunt Jemima, Boy, Porch Monkey, Spook, Mammy, Golliwogg, Nigger, Coon, Kaffir, Abeed, Monkey, Negro, Tar Baby, with Abd and Abeed being Arabic terms laden with prejudice.

These labels, steeped in racism, reflect a dark chapter in our history, illustrating how language has been weaponized to dehumanize and marginalize Black individuals.

It is ironic that despite the prevalence of mockery and belittlement toward Black people. The beauty industry spends billions yearly to replicate natural Black lip and skin tones through cosmetic surgeries and tanning products. This trend suggests that society admires the features they ridicule and discriminate against. Sadly, people are willing to invest much time, money, and effort to look like someone else instead of celebrating their individuality.

Black individuals are valued for their physical attributes but often lack genuine appreciation for their beauty and elegance. We must challenge biases and celebrate the Black heritage and humanity to create a more inclusive society.

And you shall become an[a] astonishment, a proverb, and a byword among all nations where the Lord will drive you.
Deuteronomy 28:37 (NKJV)

BROKEN WHISPERS REVISION

It's disheartening to witness the paradox of our society; the rich, diverse shades of Black women are subjected to criticism and stereotypes, while many white women worldwide attempt to replicate our natural tan despite the serious health risks involved in sun and bed tanning.

This contradiction highlights a grave misunderstanding and perpetuates harmful beauty standards, which are rooted in the false belief that Black women are "ugly" and need to be revised. We must challenge these standards and celebrate the beauty of all skin tones, including those of Black women.

The natural pigmentation of our skin, enriched with melanin, is a remarkable gift that offers unparalleled protection against the harmful effects of the sun's ultraviolet rays. This preserves the skin's radiance and youthful appearance and significantly lowers the risk of skin cancer. We must acknowledge and appreciate this inherent quality of our skin rather than feel ashamed or inferior because of it. **Remember, black don't crack!**

REVISION:

Eurocentric beauty standards harm black women's self-esteem. Empowering black women, revising broken whispers of beauty standards, and promoting diverse beauty can bring positive change.

Encourage young Black girls to embrace their unique beauty beyond the "**Barbie Doll**" ideal.

Black women can choose from various career paths that celebrate their identity and empower them to inspire the next generation.

Consider tattoo art as a career option if you love art. **Tattoo artists** create unique client designs using ink, needles, and machines. Research tattoo schools and apprenticeships to explore this career. The global tattoo market was valued at $1.89 billion in 2022 and is expected to reach $3.92 billion by 2030.

For those interested in the beauty industry, becoming a **Cosmetic Brand Founder** or **Professional Makeup Artist** can provide opportunities to create products that cater to Black women's diverse skin shades and needs.

A **Haircare Specialist** can help educate others on natural Black hair care, while a **Beauty Influencer/Blogger** can leverage social media for advocacy and trendsetting. **Dermatologists and Estheticians** can specialize in skin care tailored to melanin-rich skin.

In the fashion industry, Black women can become **Fashion Designers, Stylists, Fashion Editors/Journalists, Fashion Models, or Retail Entrepreneurs.** These careers provide opportunities to showcase the diversity of Black bodies and cultures and create apparel that makes a bold statement on runways and streets.

"Visualize a world where your permanent tan skin is highly esteemed for and appreciated."
~Phyllis Y. Whitley

EMBRACE YOUR SHINE: WHY IT'S TIME FOR ACTRESSES TO LOOK BEYOND HOLLYWOOD:

Actresses of color no longer must depend on **Hollywood**'s validation, which needs to be faster to recognize their beauty and talent. In today's world, where diversity and inclusivity are increasingly becoming essential values, people are looking for sources of entertainment that reflect these values. Thankfully, many vibrant film industries worldwide celebrate diversity and inclusivity in their productions.

Nollywood, the Nigerian film industry, is one such example. Known for producing films that showcase African culture and traditions, Nollywood has become a significant player in cinema. Similarly, **Bollywood**, the Indian film industry, is renowned for its colorful and lively productions that often incorporate elements of Indian culture and tradition. By turning to these film industries, people can enjoy entertainment that reflects their values and provides a window into different cultures and perspectives.

Supporting these industries can help actresses find empowering, culturally diverse roles. This leads to better representation of their talent, a more inclusive entertainment landscape, and inspiration for the next generation of actresses to embrace their uniqueness.

ACKNOWLEDGMENT & ACHIEVEMENT

Get ready to unleash your mind and imagination in a world where potential knows no limits! Believe in yourself, and you'll be amazed at what you can achieve. Remember the words of Napoleon Hill: "With the right mindset, any challenge can be overcome." And let's take inspiration from incredible women who have achieved their dreams despite all odds!

Black women have made their mark in various fields, from entertainment to fashion, and they continue to inspire millions worldwide with their talent, resilience, and determination to break barriers. Think of Hattie McDaniel, the trailblazing actress who won the first-ever Academy Award for a black woman, or Naomi Campbell. This iconic supermodel has shattered beauty standards and redefined fashion. And let's not forget Taraji P. Henson, the versatile actress who has earned accolades for her films and TV show performances.

These women have shown that black women are beautiful but also intelligent, creative, and powerful. Their lasting impact inspires a more just world where every black woman knows her worth. Let's join hands in this transformative journey and pave the way for future generations of extraordinary black women! Together, we can make a difference.

GOSPEL TRUTH:

Look not upon me, because I am black, Because the sun hath looked upon me...

Song of Solomon 1:6 (KJV)

PROPHETIC TRUTH POEM

In whispers of time, a revolution begins,
Celebrating diverse beauty, breaking through the spins.
More than a fight against injustice's might,
It's a song of strength, embracing what's right.

Against society's whispers, a black queen stands tall,
Her unique features are a testament to all.
From natural hairstyle to your fabulous taste,
A creation of beauty, standing in its own space.

As the world learns the roots of this grace,
Understanding and respect replace the trace.
Love the regality, a unique embrace,
In the black queen, a force, a beauty to chase.

A transformative dance fueled by self-love's light,
Breaking chains, reaching a soaring height.
Shackles dismantled, embracing what's true,
Good morning, gorgeous - a revolution in you.

PROPHETIC AFFIRMATION:

I am a masterpiece painted by the sun's kiss, my blackness a canvas of infinite grace. I love me, a declaration of strength, resilience, and unparalleled beauty. With each step, I embody the warmth of the sun's embrace, a beacon of grace in motion. I stand tall, a proud black queen, with the universe's light etching my path. I am not just seen; I shine, a luminous testament to the power I am.

Thank You, Supreme God Within!

I AM NOT MY HAIR
(SONG ARTIST: INDIA ARIE)

CHAPTER 3
MYTHS, LIES & STEREOTYPES OF BLACK WOMEN

Nappy Hair!

Black women have courageously confronted stereotypes and discrimination rooted in historical biases against their natural hair. These prejudices, tracing back to slavery, aimed to undermine Black women's beauty by deeming natural textures as undesirable.

The term "nappy," often used pejoratively, fails to honor the rich diversity of curly, kinky, and coiled hair textures that embody Black women's beauty. It's vital to dismantle these outdated notions, celebrate our Black hair's uniqueness, and recognize its inherent value.

Across various sectors, Black women endure challenges highlighting the urgent need for societal change:

- *In the corporate sector, natural Black hairstyles are unjustly deemed unprofessional.*

- *Educational institutions enforce policies that discriminate against hairstyles like afros and braids.*

- *The entertainment and media industries continue to promote Eurocentric beauty standards, marginalizing natural Black hairstyles.*

- *Fashion and beauty sectors often overlook natural Black hairstyles, favoring straight hair and perpetuating Eurocentric ideals.*

- *Sports disciplines pressure athletes to conform to hair norms that exclude natural styles.*

The enactment of the CROWN Act in California on July 3, 2019, signified a pivotal shift towards combating hair discrimination, providing protections for natural hairstyles in work and educational settings. This law has inspired similar anti-discrimination efforts nationwide, promoting acceptance of natural hairstyles like braids, locs, and twists.

Moreover, the lawsuit filed against L'Oréal and Soft Sheen Carson by four Black women in 2022 exposed the health risks associated with hair relaxer products, drawing attention to the need for safer beauty alternatives and awareness of product safety.

Advocating for the beauty of natural hair is crucial in challenging stereotypes, ensuring representation, and supporting legal protections that honor and respect the diversity of Black women's hair.

BROKEN WHISPERS REVISION

Black Queen,

It's time to take control of your hair and reject the negative stereotypes many people have about our unique hairstyles and textures. There are many myths and lies surrounding Black hair in different industries, and some women have even had to resort to legal action to fight against discrimination.

Society must move beyond its ingrained biases and accept our natural hair instead of striving to conform to Eurocentric beauty ideals reminiscent of **Ms. Barbie**. Take back your hair power by dispelling the broken whispers society has silently and sometimes broadly expressed about the unknown: your hair.

REVISION:

As Black women, we must start embracing our **natural hair** and rewriting broken whispers to confront societal pressures and injustices. By rejecting Eurocentric beauty standards and uplifting each other, we can heal from the trauma of systemic racism and reclaim our power. Together, we are unstoppable.

All Mothers of black children have the power to instill a sense of pride and self-love in their children by teaching them to embrace their natural hair and heritage. By defying stereotypes and celebrating the beauty of diversity, they are reclaiming their identity and passing on their knowledge of the intricacies of *curls, coils, braids, cornrows, twists, faux locs, and dreadlocks* to future generations. Through this act of self-acceptance, they are fostering a new generation of skilled hair specialists, black cosmetology schools, and beauty store owners who understand the cultural significance of Black hair.

Let's change the narrative around "nappy" hair and celebrate black women's natural beauty and uniqueness. Your hair is your crown and a source of pride, so embrace it joyfully. Reject Eurocentric beauty standards and celebrate your hair's versatility, strength, and cultural heritage.

Black women's hairstyle reflects an individual's rich cultural heritage and unique identity. It takes courage and confidence to showcase one's natural hair, especially in a world that often seeks conformity. Yet, this boldness is a testament to the strength and resilience of Black women everywhere.

"Prophesy greatness to yourself until greatness embodies you"
~Phyllis Y. Whitley

ACKNOWLEDGMENT & ACHIEVEMENT

The Black hair care industry has a long and vibrant history that celebrates the diverse range of textures and styles of Black hair. This legacy is owed to the tireless efforts of trailblazers like Madam CJ Walker, whose groundbreaking hair products revolutionized the industry and inspired generations of Black entrepreneurs.

The empowering "Black is Beautiful" movement of the 1960s and 1970s also played a pivotal role in promoting a positive and inclusive view of Black beauty, which helped to create a more welcoming and accepting space for Black hair care. Today, the Black achievement in the hair care industry continues to thrive, offering a wide range of products and services that cater to Black hair's unique needs and preferences.

Black women have fearlessly shattered barriers across various industries using their *natural hair* to redefine beauty and inspire inclusivity. Ursula Burns, Faith Fennidy, Viola Davis, and Tracee Ellis Ross led the charge, showcasing that Black hair is beautiful and professional. These women have inspired other Black women to celebrate their cultural pride and embrace their unique identities. Serena Williams and Simone Manuel have also overcome criticism, becoming symbols of strength and resilience. Together, we acknowledge these women have proven that authentic self-expression through the diverse beauty of Black hair is transformative, and it is time for the world to recognize and embrace it.

GOSPEL TRUTH:

How beautiful you are, my darling! Oh, how beautiful! Your eyes behind your veil are doves. Your hair is like a flock of goats descending from the hills of Gilead.

Song of Solomon 4:1 (NIV)

PROPHETIC TRUTH POEM

I am not my hair; my hair is me. In the whispers of each texture, a tale unfolds,
Breaking stereotypes, a story of courage untold.
No longer confined to Eurocentric decree,
Black women rise, their true selves set free.

Revel in the beauty of textures diverse,
Celebrate self in an empowering verse.
"Don't be threatened by my crown, it's my queen's expression,
A declaration of pride, devoid of suppression.
Braids, twists, and dreadlocks, in majestic procession,
Showcase the depth of our ancestral connection.

In a world of shades, diverse and free,
My strands weave tales of identity.
Curls, coils, braids, and dreadlocks, a unique decree,
Rooted in strength, they're my legacy.
In every tress, a truth to see,
My hair is a symbol of my queenly decree.

PROPHETIC AFFIRMATION:

Today, I affirm my power and purpose. I am cultivating a mindset of growth and resilience, transforming challenges into opportunities. I elevate my consciousness to manifest dreams into reality, embodying the strength and pride of my heritage in every aspect of my being.

I master self-expression, boldly wearing my crown of confidence, a testament to my journey and resilience. In my hair, my legacy thrives, a mosaic of pride and identity.

I stand tall, unbounded by norms, my spirit free. I receive blessings and opportunities gracefully, claiming my space as a queen in this vast world. Today, I radiate strength, grace, and sovereignty.

Thank You, Supreme God Within!

BABY GOT BACK
(SONG ARTIST: SIR MIX-A-LOT)

CHAPTER 4
MYTHS, LIES & STEREOTYPES OF BLACK WOMEN

Big Butt!

We find ourselves at a crossroads of reflection and change in a world too often shadowed by the remnants of a painful history. The legacy of human zoos, where individuals were objectified and dehumanized, casts a long shadow over our collective consciousness. These exhibitions, whether as "Negro Villages" in Europe and America or showcasing the indigenous "Andaman People" in India, revealed a profound misunderstanding and disrespect for human dignity.

At the heart of this dark era lies the story of Sarah "Saartjie" Baartman, a 20-year-old South African woman whose body, particularly her protuberant buttock, was cruelly exploited for entertainment and dehumanization. This divergence from European beauty ideals subjected her and many black women to profound disrespect.

Exhibited in cages at sideshows, they were displayed like mere curiosities to white audiences, an indignity akin to objectification. Intriguingly, the features that "white European race" people once ridiculed and sexually exploited are now coveted by many white women, who undergo plastic surgery for butt enhancements and/or also seek cosmetics like buttock injections to replicate the black women's butts that were once disparaged.

The return of Saartjie Baartman's remains to South Africa in 2002, a gesture led by Nelson Mandela, marks a significant step towards acknowledging and healing the wounds of the past. It is a potent reminder of the ongoing need for dignity, respect, and understanding.

Yet, the enduring impact of these historical injustices subtly affects today's perceptions of beauty and self-worth, perpetuating beauty standards rooted in a colonial past and challenging our sense of identity and acceptance. This complex history, underscored in Dalton Jr.'s "Hebrews to Negroes" (2015), necessitates a critical reevaluation of beauty standards.

As we tackle enduring biases, the irony of non-black individuals seeking features associated with African heritage through surgery highlights our complex beauty standards. We must actively challenge stereotypes, embrace inclusivity, and celebrate our diverse heritage, moving beyond history to acknowledge every individual's inherent worth.

BROKEN WHISPERS REVISION

"Broken Whispers Revision" aims to empower and inspire change by confronting the harmful stereotypes of black women perpetuated by various industries. Let's avoid judging women based on their physical attributes and instead focus on their strength and resilience because that truly matters—uplifting women and celebrating their inner strength.

I completely understand how frustrating it must be for people who don't fit into the traditional beauty standards set by Hollywood and the beauty and fashion industry. It's important to recognize and celebrate the beauty of African heritage and empower black women to embrace their unique diversity.

REVISION:

Our **inner thoughts and feelings** impact our bodies. We must care for ourselves and our families through healthy habits, promoting self-love, and positive body image. Learn which foods help and which harm, and try meditation and prayer to reduce stress and improve overall health.

Empower yourself with holistic remedies - mindfulness, exercise, healthy eating, good sleep, positive thinking, yoga, meditation, aromatherapy and massage. Live your best life by incorporating these remedies into your daily routine.

1. **Herbalism for Self-Love:** Embrace herbalism to nurture your body and mind, using nature's remedies to promote a positive body image and self-esteem.
2. **Yoga & African Dance:** Embodied Confidence. Combine the grounding practice of yoga with the vibrant energy of African dance to celebrate your body's movement and build self-confidence.
3. **Cooking Cultural Foods:** Culinary Self-Expression. Explore cooking healthy traditional foods as a form of self-care and cultural expression. Connect with your roots and foster body positivity.
4. **Meditation Music & Colon Hydrotherapy for Wellness:** Integrate meditation music for mental well-being and colon hydrotherapy for physical health to affirm your right to holistic health and vitality.

Set higher goals for yourself and your children by owning fashion companies, clothing lines, modeling agencies, health spas, sports clubs, and healthy restaurants. Promote positive body image and strive to be the best version of ourselves and the women in our community to create a positive change in the world.

"Your body is a garden that flourishes with God's food, not man-made."
~Phyllis Y. Whitley

ACKNOWLEDGMENT & ACHIEVEMENT

Remarkable black women who overcame adversity and revised their broken whispers are genuinely inspiring. Lizzo, the Grammy award-winning singer and rapper, has used her music to promote body positivity and self-love, encouraging fans to embrace themselves just as they are. Serena Williams, the tennis legend, has broken barriers in sports, challenged stereotypes, and paved the way for future generations of female athletes.

Ashley Graham, the model and entrepreneur, has been a vocal advocate for inclusivity and diversity in the fashion industry, pushing for more representation of all body types and sizes. Gabourey Sidibe, the actress and director, has been a trailblazer in Hollywood. She advocates for diversity and inclusivity in the entertainment industry through her platform.

Octavia Spencer, the Academy Award-winning actress, has always valued talent over appearance, speaking out against discrimination in Hollywood and advocating for more opportunities for underrepresented groups. Danielle Brooks, the actress and singer, has been a powerful voice for body diversity in entertainment, promoting self-love and body acceptance for all.

These women have significantly impacted their respective fields, serving as role models for many and inspiring countless others to pursue their dreams and make a positive difference in the world.

GOSPEL TRUTH:

How beautiful are your feet in sandals,
O prince's daughter!
The curves of your thighs are like jewels,
The work of the hands of a skillful workman.
Your navel is a rounded goblet;
It lacks no blended beverage.
Your waist is a heap of wheat
Set about with lilies.

Song of Solomon 7:1-2 (NKJV)

PROPHETIC TRUTH POEM

I am fearfully and wonderfully made, you see,
Quiet the jealous naysayers, for in God's image, we've been laid.
They whisper about our big butt, yet I stand free.
Empowering black women to embrace their own,
With boundless strength, recognizing my worth is known.

Celebrating beauty, our African genetics we exalt,
Defying standards that sought to suppress, halt.
In this unwavering journey, hand in hand, side by side,
In a world of self-love, we stand with resilience and pride as our guide.

Shapely buttocks, we declare, do not define our space,
It's in self-acceptance that our spirits passionately embrace.
For beauty's defined by the kindest of hearts, no straying off track,
We boldly proclaim in every black woman's figure,
"Baby Got Back"

PROPHETIC AFFIRMATION:

With every curve of my backside, I am a celebration of distinctiveness, a rich legacy of African strength coursing through me. Turning away from societal molds, I am confidently journeying on the path of self-love. My value lies in my kindness, my truth in my authenticity. I affirm, "I am my beauty, inside and out," shaped by divine craftsmanship. Fearlessly and wonderfully made, I am enveloped in divine love, a radiant symbol of resilience and grace.

Thank You, Supreme God Within!

WIDE NOSE FULL LIPS
(SONG ARTIST: SUCH)

CHAPTER 5
MYTHS, LIES & STEREOTYPES OF BLACK WOMEN

Big Nose & Lips!

It's no secret that our society holds a harmful and misguided belief that black women's unique facial features, such as their noses and lips, are somehow less attractive. This perception is rooted in historical biases and perpetuates damaging stereotypes. However, it's ironic that non-black individuals often spend a fortune on **lip fillers** and facial enhancements in an attempt to emulate the very features that black women are criticized for. This stark contrast highlights the inherent beauty of these features and challenges the negative portrayal of black women. We must acknowledge and celebrate the beauty in all women, regardless of their race or physical features.

Black women have been criticized for their noses and lips, leading to self-acceptance issues. Some opt for surgery to fit society's narrow beauty standards. However, nose and lip sizes vary across Africa, reflecting our diverse ancestry. West Africans have the most prominent noses, North Africans the narrowest. This variability is genetic and shaped by the hot African climate, necessitating a wider nose for air intake. Over time, this trait has become symbolic of African heritage.

The deliberate act of historical erasure is a poignant example of how African heritage is systematically diminished. Removing the **Sphinx's** nose and erasing African contributions from history perpetuates a damaging pattern of erasure that mirrors today's struggles with identity and representation. We must recognize the importance of preserving diverse histories and the contributions of all cultures to build a more inclusive and equitable future.

Our facial features, especially our noses, deeply connect to our ancestors and symbolize a rich history. It's essential to embrace these features, understand their significance, and challenge misconceptions and stereotypes. Celebrating our features as emblems of strength, resilience, and beauty urges a world where everyone can stand tall, be proud of their heritage, and be confident in their beauty.

Recent research from the National Library of Medicine underscores a fascinating shift in societal beauty standards. Fuller lips are now celebrated as emblems of sensuality, youth, and vitality. This burgeoning appreciation has sparked a surge in demand for lip enhancements, ironically affirming the inherent beauty of features once marginalized and stereotyped, especially in Black women.

Features like prominent lips and noses, previously subjected to bias, have become desirable traits. This contradiction contributes to the booming **Botox** industry in the U.S., which generates nearly $1.5 billion annually.

The irony deepens as non-Black individuals pursue cosmetic procedures to replicate the very traits of Black women's natural beauty, underscoring a long-overdue recognition of their allure.

The pressure on Black women to alter their appearance highlights the need for introspection on beauty perceptions. Conversations celebrating African features, like the African nose, are crucial to combat negative attitudes and promote self-acceptance. Change is urgent.

"Revise your inner whispers for a different prophetic view."

~Phyllis Y. Whitley

BROKEN WHISPERS REVISION

Black women have been subjected to Eurocentric beauty standards for far too long, causing them to feel inadequate and unattractive. But it's time for a revision of Broken Whispers. By embracing their natural beauty and rejecting these standards, Black women can begin their healing journey and empower themselves, starting with these powerful whispers.

REVISION:

Broken whispers are negative self-talk experienced by Black women due to societal pressure. Celebrating their unique features promotes self-love and acceptance, helping them overcome self-doubt and promoting inclusivity. Here are some ways to implement this strategy:

1. **Seek Positive Representation and Education.**

Engage with media, art, and fashion that celebrate African features and highlight Black beauty in its myriad forms. This rejects Eurocentric beauty standards and fosters pride and appreciation for natural beauty.

2. **Cultivate Self-Affirmation and Mindful Acceptance.**

To improve mental wellness and develop self-love, practice daily self-affirmation by celebrating your natural facial features. Repeat phrases such as "My features are a legacy of strength." This can positively impact Black women's internal dialogue and promote compassionate acceptance of their beauty.

3. Build and Participate in Supportive Communities.

Join safe communities of Black women to celebrate their beauty and achievements. These communities provide collective empowerment, enhance self-esteem, and counter harmful beauty standards.

4. Embrace and Share Knowledge.

Learn and share the history and cultural significance of African facial features and hairstyles to dispel myths and enrich understanding. This can lead to a shift towards recognizing and respecting diversity in your community and social circles.

Empowering yourself to celebrate your natural beauty can help you break free from restrictive beauty standards and create a future where your unique features are celebrated without limitations.

ACKNOWLEDGMENT & ACHIEVEMENT

Black women need to embrace their unique beauty and reject narrow beauty standards. Celebrating cultural heritage and empowering oneself should be a priority. Unrealistic Eurocentric beauty standards should be abandoned in favor of simplicity. Instead of striving to fit into the mold of the masses, we should rejoice in our differences and accept our individual beauty.

With her 23 Grand Slam titles and unwavering determination, Serena Williams has become an icon for aspiring athletes worldwide, inspiring them to break free from the limitations of societal norms and strive for greatness. Simone Biles, with her unparalleled strength and grace, has redefined what it means to be a gymnast and has inspired a generation of young girls to pursue their goals fearlessly.

Lupita Nyong'o, with her trailblazing career and powerful advocacy for diversity and representation, has become a symbol of hope and inspiration for people of all backgrounds, encouraging them to celebrate their individuality and embrace their unique perspectives.

These women embody the best of us: courage, resilience, and commitment to a more inclusive world. Their self-love and acceptance of their unique features inspire us to celebrate differences. Let's celebrate everyone's beauty, regardless of size, shape, or color, to fix our broken whispers.

GOSPEL TRUTH:

Your neck is like an ivory tower.
Your eyes are the pools of Heshbon
by the gate of Bath Rabbim.
Your nose is like the tower of Lebanon
looking toward Damascus.
Your head crowns you like Mount Carmel.
Your hair is like royal tapestry;
the king is held captive by its tresses.

Song of Songs 7:4-5 (NIV)

PROPHETIC TRUTH POEM

In the whispers of life, my features are a story that can't
be cut out,
A narrative of strength whispered about in shouts.
Celebrating our uniqueness, our spirits enshrined,
Beyond the shadows, misconceptions are left behind.

Reflected in the mirror, a testament of might,
Our souls dancing, bathed in divine light.
In the depths of our essence, the truth unfurls,
A spiritual beauty transcends the physical world.

On inclusivity's path, we courageously sail,
Embracing each other, where no dream is frail.
Our spirits soar: in diversity, we delight,
A symphony of features, shining ever so bright.

Against the old standards, our radiance takes flight,
Champions of our stories, in the darkness, we ignite.

The beauty of our heritage, a guiding light so pure,
Where **Wide Nose Full Lips**,
their whispers reassure.

PROPHETIC AFFIRMATION:

Today and always, I celebrate the beauty of my heritage, cherishing my broad nose and full lips. I confidently navigate life's pathways, shining with divine light. Today and always, I honor my physical features as a testament to divine craftsmanship, embracing my timeless beauty and strength shaped by God's imagination.

Thank You, Supreme God Within!

OREO
(SONG ARTIST: RICO NASTY)

CHAPTER 6
MYTHS, LIES & STEREOTYPES OF BLACK WOMEN

Oreo/Mulatto!

In the fabric of society, the words we choose to describe each other hold immense power, often reflecting deeper societal attitudes and biases. When a Black woman is derogatorily labeled as an "Oreo," it does more than just assign a hurtful nickname; it perpetuates harmful stereotypes that cut to the core of an individual's racial and cultural identity. This term, suggesting someone is "black on the outside, white on the inside," denies the complexity of racial identity, reducing it to a matter of superficial traits and stereotypical behaviors. It's a label that stings, suggesting individuals cannot be true to their racial and cultural heritage if they do not conform to narrow, preconceived expectations.

Equally troubling is the use of the term "mulatto," a word steeped in a painful history that dates to the era of slavery and segregation. This outdated and profoundly inappropriate label carries the weight of a past when racial categorization was wielded as a tool of division and discrimination. To use such a term today is to perpetuate notions of racial purity inadvertently and to foster a divisive and harmful view of racial identity.

The brutal legacy of slavery casts a long shadow over the present, particularly in the harrowing reality that Black and Indigenous female slaves were subjected to rape by their enslavers. These abhorrent acts, committed with utter disregard for the humanity of these women—many of whom were mothers and wives—have left indelible scars. The children born of these violent unions, despite their mixed heritage, were still relegated to the status of slaves. This dark chapter in history is a significant factor in the diversity of skin tones and hair textures among African Americans today, a testament to a past marred by unspeakable cruelty and injustice.

This phenomenon is not unique to the United States. Still, it is also part of the history of Spanish colonies in Central and South America and the Caribbean, contributing to the rich tapestry of racial and cultural identities in places like Cuba, Puerto Rico, and the Dominican Republic.

These narratives and terms, steeped in prejudice and pain, underscore the need for a profound and empathetic reassessment of how we speak about race and identity. They remind us of the importance of moving beyond simplistic and harmful stereotypes to embrace a more inclusive and nuanced understanding of identity.

It's about recognizing history's enduring impact on present-day realities and working together to foster a society where every individual is respected and valued for who they are, free from the shadows of derogatory labels and the pain they inflict. In doing so, we affirm our shared humanity and take steps toward healing the wounds of the past, paving the way for a more compassionate and inclusive future.

BROKEN WHISPERS REVISION

It is essential to acknowledge the problematic history of our ancestors. Still, it's also heartening to see that the majority of **multiracial and biracial** children born today are a product of love between interracial parents.

However, it is disheartening to know that these children still face stereotypes and prejudices that need to be debunked through continuous efforts. Remember that you are a unique and beautiful individual with limitless potential waiting to be unleashed. Please know that you are not alone; together, we can work towards a more inclusive and accepting world.

REVISION:

To empower themselves and challenge societal boxes, mixed-race Black women can adopt four empowering strategies that promote healing broken whispers.

Firstly, you can cultivate a supportive community that values diversity and inclusivity. This community can provide a space for sharing broken whispers and revision stories and building a foundation of mutual respect and empowerment.

Secondly, mixed-race Black women can celebrate their diverse cultural backgrounds by delving into and embracing their heritage. By doing so, they an dispel stereotypes and educate others about the beauty of diversity, enriching their sense of self and contributing to a more nuanced societal understanding of identity.

Thirdly, advocating for authentic representation across all spheres of society is essential in "healing broken whispers." Mixed-race Black women can alter perceptions and inspire a more inclusive representation by challenging monolithic narratives and demanding accurate portrayals. This advocacy is a powerful form of "broken whispers revision," paving the way for future generations to see themselves reflected in the stories that shape our world.

Finally, prioritizing personal reflection and self-care is crucial to "healing broken whispers." Mixed-race Black women can personally engage in "broken whispers revision" through mindfulness, creative expression, and self-affirmation. This nurtures an inner sanctuary of peace and self-acceptance, reinforcing the importance of self-love and the rejection of limiting stereotypes.

Multicultural and biracial Black women must embrace their unique tapestry of cultural identities and navigate confidently by following these strategies. We stand with them and challenge societal boxes to promote inclusivity, respect, and equality. It's time to celebrate diversity and empower everyone to be authentic.

"I need to use my full potential within to manifest unlimited results."
~Phyllis Y. Whitley

ACKNOWLEDGMENT & ACHIEVEMENT

Black women are breaking free from labels and stereotypes, embracing cultural fluidity, and transcending societal boundaries. Let's celebrate their fantastic journey of achievement.
We honor extraordinary women, each born to parents of mixed-race backgrounds, who've made their mark in different industries and left a powerful legacy for generations to come!

From the trailblazing Halle Berry, who achieved a significant milestone in Hollywood by becoming the first black woman to win an Academy Award for Best Actress, to the remarkable Meghan Markle, who broke racial barriers in the British monarchy, Kamala Harris is another inspiring woman who has made history as the first female, first Black, and first South Asian Vice President of the United States.

Let's not forget about Mariah Carey, the multi-platinum-selling singer and songwriter known for her incredible vocal range, or Misty Copeland, who achieved a historic milestone when she became the American Ballet Theatre's first African American female principal dancer. Additionally, Maya

Rudolph, the versatile actress, comedian, and musician renowned for her humor and talent, and Soledad O'Brien, the accomplished journalist and documentarian who's covered significant global events.

Finally, we have Jurnee Smollett, the talented actress recognized for her captivating performances in film and television, and Rashida Jones, the successful actress, writer, and producer known for her contributions to the entertainment industry.

Your mixed-race heritage does not limit your achievements; their accomplishments are exemplary and a testament to the value of embracing cultural fluidity. They have shattered broken whispers and barriers, fostered connections within and beyond the black community, and motivated a new generation to challenge stereotypes and strive for greatness!

GOSPEL TRUTH:

But the Lord said to Samuel, "Do not consider his appearance or his height, for I have rejected him. The Lord does not look at the things people look at. People look at the outward appearance, but the Lord looks at the heart.

1 Samuel 16:7 (NIV)

PROPHETIC TRUTH POEM

*In a world where "**Oreo**" cuts and "Mulatto" stings,*
Black women stand with the might their heritage brings.
Pioneers they become, stereotypes to dismantle,
In their manifold selves, a history ample.

Do not be swayed, for each hue reveals,
Traces of Africa, through time, are concealed.
Through slave trades, their essence remained,
In every shade, their ancestry claimed.

Fluidity's not frailty, but strength unveiled,
In their souls, dignity is forever detailed.
From the shadows of bias, they step into the light,
With courage drawn from heritage, ever so bright.

Through strength and grace, the paths they carve,
Black women's journey, in triumph they starve.
Embracing all facets, they stand tall, they breathe,
In their identity's power, they fervently believe.

In society's weave, the terms we cast,
Reflect deeper biases and shadows they cast.
"**Oreo**," "Mulatto," words that divide,
Ignore the richness within, the depth they hide.

Let's shift our speech, uplift, and unite,
Honor each story, each plight.
For in every Black woman, a world unfurled,
A mosaic of identities around the globe.

PROPHETIC AFFIRMATION:

Today, in every fabulous way, I am proud of my heritage and all that it brings. I am breaking down stereotypes and embracing my diverse self. Every tone and color reflects my ancestry.

I value diversity and broaden my horizons by viewing things from different angles. I am resilient, and my story is important. I am strong, and I fight for my beliefs. I am stepping out of the shadows of bias and embracing my identity's power. I am proud of who I am, and I stand with confidence.

Thank You, Supreme God Within!

NO MORE DRAMA
(SONG ARTIST: MARY J. BLIGE)

CHAPTER 7
MYTHS, LIES & STEREOTYPES OF BLACK WOMEN

Drama Queen!

The portrayal of Black women through the Sapphire Caricature as rude, loud, malicious, and overbearing is not only a gross misrepresentation but also a harmful social control mechanism. This stereotype, which paints African American women as the "Angry Black Woman" (ABW) in media, serves to demean and dehumanize them, enforcing a societal expectation for Black women to remain passive and unseen.

Such depictions are not isolated; they are part of a broader narrative that includes the Jezebel and Mammy paradigms, painting Black femininity as either *hypersexual, boisterous, aggressive, or self-sacrificing and nurturing.* These stereotypes have tangible impacts on the lives of Black girls and women today, influencing how they are perceived and treated by society, including in educational settings where behaviors deviating from traditional femininity may be unfairly penalized.

This resilience originates from the painful history of slavery, where Black men were forcibly separated from their families and stripped of dignity. Black women have observed this pattern repeating over generations. In the absence of their Black kings, they've taken on the roles of both man and woman within their families, thrust into survivor mode. Their assertiveness and resilience are born of necessity, a response to centuries of marginalization and injustice.

Labeling Black women as "drama queens" further simplifies Black women's responses to adversity as mere overemotional reactions, ignoring the systemic injustices that inform their responses. This stereotype fails to appreciate the historical context of their resilience, which often stems from a place of protection and defense for themselves and their loved ones.

Before jumping to judgments or clinging to stereotypes, it's crucial to approach with compassion and seek understanding. Recognizing and valuing Black women's diverse experiences and individuality is a step forward in moving beyond reductive labels and towards a more inclusive and empathetic society.

Their strength and assertiveness, often misconstrued as unnecessary drama, deserve to be seen for what they are: admirable qualities born of necessity and resilience. Embracing this perspective is essential in celebrating the full humanity of Black women, free from the confines of societal expectations and prejudice.

BROKEN WHISPERS REVISION

Queens, it's time to take action and empower Black women. We can start by challenging societal perceptions and dispelling harmful myths.

REVISION:

Broken Whispers Revision is a lifestyle change that promotes holistic well-being. It focuses on replacing harmful noise with strategies for effective communication and self-expression. The program emphasizes lifestyle and dietary changes to improve physical and mental health.

1. There are many ways to express oneself creatively, but two popular methods are **poetry** and dancing. Poetry is a form of literary expression often involving language to convey emotions, thoughts, or experiences. On the other hand, dancing is a physical expression that expresses feelings and ideas through movement and rhythm. Both forms of expression can be powerful and allow individuals to communicate uniquely and meaningfully.

2. One can practice **prayer** and **meditation** and spend time in nature to foster spiritual and holistic well-being. These activities help connect individuals with themselves, others, and their environment. By making these practices a part of their daily routine, individuals can achieve a more fulfilling life, leading to greater peace and well-being.

3. Try adopting a plant-based, pescatarian, or keto diet to improve your health and mental clarity. These diets focus on whole foods like fruits, vegetables, whole grains, nuts, and seeds. The keto diet is low-carb, high-fat, aiming to shift your body into ketosis. The pescatarian diet includes fish, seafood, and plant-based foods. Healthy nutrition can benefit your **physical and mental health**, align with your values, and promote self-expression and resilience.

4. Consider seeking the guidance of a spiritual counselor, mentor, or coach to aid you in your quest for spiritual growth and enlightenment. These experienced professionals can provide valuable support, inspiration, and direction as you explore your beliefs, values, and purpose. They can help you overcome obstacles, cultivate inner peace, and unlock your full spiritual potential by tapping into the wisdom, love, and light within you.

By integrating these strategies, including dietary choices that reflect a commitment to health and ethical living, Black women can communicate effectively and express themselves authentically. This **holistic** approach supports individual well-being and contributes to broader societal change.

"Use your mind's power to achieve your desires while carefully guiding your senses."
~Phyllis Y. Whitley

ACKNOWLEDGMENT & ACHIEVEMENT

It is essential to acknowledge that many black women develop a protective outer shell to guard themselves against repeated heartbreaks and disappointments from those around them. However, beneath that exterior lies a heart of gold. By treating these women with kindness and respect, you can build a meaningful and long-lasting friendship that will be rewarding for both of you.

These black women have turned their struggles and broken whispers into a positive impact in society:

1. **Michelle Obama** - As the former First Lady of the United States, Michelle Obama is celebrated for her advocacy and accomplishments, warmth, genuine smile, and compassionate nature. Her public engagements and speeches often reflect her kind-heartedness and commitment to uplifting communities. Her initiatives, such as "Let's Move!" for children's health and her focus on education, showcase her dedication to making a positive impact with grace and empathy.

2. **Oprah Winfrey** - Oprah Winfrey, a media mogul, philanthropist, and public figure, is renowned for her empathetic and warm-hearted approach to life. Her groundbreaking talk show was a platform for healing, understanding, and celebrating human experiences, often highlighting her laughter, kindness, and generosity. Through her philanthropic efforts, Oprah has touched the lives of many across the globe, embodying the spirit of giving and compassion.

3. **Maya Angelou**—The late Maya Angelou, a celebrated poet, writer, and civil rights activist, was known for her powerful voice and gentle spirit. Her literary works and public speeches often conveyed messages of hope, resilience, and kindness, touching the hearts of many. Angelou's infectious smile, laughter, profound wisdom, and good heart made her a beloved figure whose legacy continues to inspire kindness and understanding.

These women left their mark on the world with their achievements and embodiment of kindness, warmth, and genuine benevolence.

GOSPEL TRUTH:

She opens her mouth with wisdom,
And on her tongue is the law of kindness.

Proverbs 31:26 (NKJV)

PROPHETIC TRUTH POEM

Ignore my roar, whispers of strength we share,
Each burden carried with a strength so rare,
Through trials and tribulations, we have seen,
Emerges resilience, a spirit so keen.

With grace and courage, we rise to the scene,
Don't judge my whispers; let understanding glean,
Defying expectations with hearts serene,
No longer bound by roles, no longer unseen,

We shatter stereotypes; our worth, we glean.
For we are not defined by any screen,
Not just a "drama queen," as they may deem,
Our souls are vibrant, our spirits agleam,

United, we rise in a luminous beam,
No more drama*; let our truth stream.*

PROPHETIC AFFIRMATION:

I am the master of my mind. Therefore, I am a fabulous queen, and my name carries power. With unwavering confidence, I manifest my desires guided by divine wisdom. I release drama and radiate realism and laughter, attracting blessings effortlessly. I trust my infinite potential in perfect harmony with the universe. I am a force of positivity, creating a life of beauty, purpose, and abundance.

Thank You, Supreme God Within!

BBW (BEAUTIFUL BLACK WOMAN)
(SONG ARTIST: REASON)

CHAPTER 8
MYTHS, LIES & STEREOTYPES OF BLACK WOMEN

Undesirable!

As a society, we must approach the stereotypes surrounding Black women with empathy and compassion. We need to recognize the depth of these issues and strive for a more inclusive understanding. It's deeply concerning that the narrative that single Black women are undesirable persists despite it being rooted in societal prejudices that unfairly categorize them based on race, skin tone, and features.

These stereotypes are harmful and can cause much pain for the women they target. Understanding that research uncovers a multifaceted reality that contradicts these harmful stereotypes is vital. Our goal should be to advocate for a world that treats women fairly and impartially, ensuring they receive equitable treatment.

Numerous studies have shown that physical attractiveness stereotypes are applied differently to women of different races, with white women receiving preferential treatment over Black women with darker skin and African features. This bias contributes to discrimination against Black women in society and relationships.

Furthermore, Black women's educational and professional achievements are often underappreciated and undervalued. Even though almost twice as many Black women graduate from college as Black men, they still face stereotypes that undermine their desirability. Many college-educated Black women are more likely to marry partners with less education or lower earnings, which reflects societal inequalities. This text disputes the false notion that they are ineligible for marriage or don't improve one's status.

The demographic imbalance in the Black community, where the number of Black males is 91 for every 100 Black females, is influenced by various socio-economic factors. This issue further highlights the need for a broader societal shift in perception and value.

Additionally, the tendency for Black men to marry outside their race more frequently than Black women contributes to the unique challenges Black women face in finding partners who match their achievements and aspirations. As a result, Black women often encounter difficulties in finding suitable partners and may feel pressured to marry someone outside their educational level.

We must break free from harmful stereotypes and recognize the resilience, beauty, and worth of Black women.

BROKEN WHISPERS REVISION

Black women often face marginalization and undervaluation due to societal norms. Practicing **self-love** and respect and pursuing equality are essential to overcome these limitations. Here are pivotal strategies for revising broken whispers: navigate and challenge societal expectations to assert your rightful place as a **desired**, respected, and equal individual.

REVISION:

Diversifying Love and Relationships: Society often fails to recognize the full extent of Black women's desirability in love and relationships. However, the misconception that Black women are less sought after is false. They receive genuine passion and interest globally, proving their broad appeal. Encouraging Black women to embrace love in all its forms, regardless of boundaries, challenges the limiting narrative.

Correcting Media Misrepresentations: Mainstream media often ignores Black women in interracial and intercultural relationships, which distorts perceptions of their desirability. Promoting representations of their varied and rich love lives can shift public perception and highlight that they are deeply loved by partners of all backgrounds.

Leveraging Maternal Influence: Mothers tremendously influence young Black girls' self-image - they have the power to teach their daughters that they are not mere backups, but unique individuals destined for greatness as queens. Similarly, they can teach their sons to respect the beauty and strength of Black women. By instilling a deep sense of self-worth and confidence, mothers prepare their children to fearlessly face the world, knowing they are valuable and deserving of love and respect. This instills a critical lesson of originality and dignity, essential for their growth and development.

Redefining Societal Standards: Society often views Black women through stereotypes and unrealistic expectations. It's time to challenge these constructs and advocate for a narrative recognizing their diverse excellence. Through community engagement, education, and personal stories, we can break down **false perceptions**, revealing the strength, beauty, and intelligence that have long been overshadowed.

Mindful Practices and Mental Health Care: Black women can cultivate inner peace through **mindful practices** like *prayer, meditation, yoga, and journaling.* Professional mental health care and support groups provide a safe space to heal from racial and gender-specific traumas. Prioritizing mental health care is an empowering act of self-love. Take care of your mind to live your best life.

Cultural Connection and Heritage Appreciation: Black women can find strength and healing by connecting with their African heritage. Celebrating traditions and history and participating in community rituals fosters belonging and pride. This **connection** to roots and ancestry counters societal devaluation, nurturing the soul and reinforcing positive self-image.

Black women possess intrinsic worth and beauty that should be acknowledged and celebrated. By embracing empowering strategies and the tool of broken whispers revision, they can pave a path towards a future where society recognizes and appreciates this truth. Let us join in this journey of empowerment, not just for personal growth but also for the transformation of society's fabric. Reclaiming the Throne of **Self-Worth** is within reach.

"As long as you see your promised land within, it will attach itself to you"
~Phyllis Y. Whitley

ACKNOWLEDGMENT & ACHIEVEMENT

Let's take a moment to honor the remarkable men who have chosen to marry **Black queens** and break down stereotypes. Their choices prove that love knows no color boundaries and inspire us to embrace diversity and acceptance. This list includes some truly inspiring individuals who have significantly impacted their respective fields.

These include Angela of Liechtenstein, recognized for her philanthropic work and social activism. Lei von Habsburg of Austria is a renowned artist and designer. Keisha Omilana of Nigeria is a successful entrepreneur and advocate for women's empowerment. Nyanut von Habsburg of Austria is a model and humanitarian. 'Masenate Mohato Seeiso of Lesotho is the queen consort of Lesotho and has championed various causes related to education and healthcare.

Cecile de Massy of Monaco (now divorced) is a businesswoman and founder of several charitable organizations. Emma Thynn (Viscountess Weymouth) is a philanthropist and animal rights activist. Sylvia of Buganda is a princess and advocate for women's rights. Ariana Austin Makonnen of Ethiopia is an attorney and philanthropist. Last but not least, Meghan, the

Duchess of Sussex, a member of the British royal family and a former actress. She is known for her advocacy for women's rights and her humanitarian work.

These unions defy stereotypes, inspiring us to honor Black women's beauty and strength. They rise above societal limits, rewriting their narratives and showcasing boundless potential. It's a call to celebrate their uniqueness and strive for an inclusive, equitable future that values their diverse strengths and contributions.

GOSPEL TRUTH:

Her children rise up and call her blessed;
Her husband also, and he praises her:
Many daughters have done well,
But you excel them all.
Charm is deceitful and beauty is passing,
But a woman who fears the Lord, she shall be
praised.

Proverbs 31:28-30 (NKJV)

PROPHETIC TRUTH POEM

In dawn's light, truths emerge,
In a world dim, Black women surge.
History's script in their stride,
Against narrow voices, they abide.
Stereotypes cast shadows wide,
Yet, in resilience, they take pride.
Not for society's eye, but ancestral call,
Through education and community, they stand tall.

Media's lens shifts, now seeing clear,
Their accomplishments, and dreams, are held dear.
In every step, grace and desire combine,
Defying darkness, their spirits shine.

Hear this ode, let praises bound,
For in Black women, a universe is found.
"**Beautiful Black Woman**," we sing with glee,
In essence, the world sees freedom as key.

PROPHETIC AFFIRMATION:

I am transcending stereotypes unbound by societal preconceptions. I am beyond desirable; I am cherished and celebrated for my unique beauty and strength. I am rewriting my story with grace and pride. I am consciousness, a vessel of boundless potential. I am manifesting dreams into reality with my vivid imagination. I am every deliberate thought shaping my destiny. I am not an option; I am a treasure, embodying inherent worth.

Thank You, Supreme God Within!

Conclusion Prophetic Poem:

*Refuse to be a canvas for society's cruel **experiment**,*
A test on mind, body, and soul—this we must lament.

*Our **ancestors**, stripped of words, heritage lost in flames,*
Bearing slave owners' names, enduring unspeakable waves of shame.

*Families **torn apart**, a servant mindset instilled,*
Yet through centuries of silence, their strength never killed.

Today, they assault our senses, a continuous fight,
*With financial strains and **mental battles** challenging our might.*

*In bodies once marred by **brutality's** unforgiving hand,*
Raped and reduced, treated less than the land.

*Today, they aim to **poison** us with food, vaccines, and prescription drugs,*
A sinister test, our essence, they wish to kill.

Our souls, once free, now tangled in webs they spun,
*Forced to worship foreign gods, our true **prophets** were shunned.*

*Today, our **spirits** are plundered; in pews and halls, we kneel,*
Our faith in leaders, not God, is a wound that won't heal.

Yet, amid this darkness, a glimmering light of hope,
Our ancestors' resilience and legacy help us cope.

***Cursed** when from God we strayed, yet His promise remains true,*
***Return to Him**, reclaim the land of milk and honey, renew.*

*So, let us break free from chains, from **history's painful scars**,*
Reconnect with our Creator and reach for the stars.

In God's blessings, we find strength, a path divinely set,
*Claiming our **promised land**, a future without regret.*

This journey, though fraught with trials, with God we'll overcome,
*Returning to **our roots**, our divine anthem hums.*

For in His embrace, we find freedom, love, and peace,
*A return to Him, where all **trials cease**.*

PROPHETIC AFFIRMATION:

I declare today that I am chosen and destined for greatness. The Universe treasures me as part of a sacred collective, a chosen race, and a royal priesthood. I have been skillfully crafted with divine precision and love, I am joyful to celebrate my creation. I am a testament to the marvelous works of the Divine, fearfully and wonderfully made. My soul recognizes this truth; I am empowered with unshakeable peace, purpose, and strength.

Thank You, Supreme God Within!

PROPHETIC PRAYER

Dear Lord

I humbly step into Your presence with an open heart, ready to embrace the fullness of Your love. Today, I made a conscious choice to forgive and release all my naysayers and dissolve every negative stereotype, myth, and lie about my black essence.

I now understand that I am fearfully and wonderfully made, equipped to conquer every obstacle with the greatness predestined.

Drawing closer to You through prayer and meditation makes every challenge a stepping stone treasured by the Universe.
Reflecting on Your divine works, I am prepared to live in my promised land as I help others reach theirs, empowered with peace, purpose, and patience. Knowing the truth has set me free.
Amen.

EMPOWERING LEGACIES
CELEBRATING BLACK WOMEN'S IMPACT

Black Women Chefs!

Carla Hall, Sunny Anderson, Lorraine Pascale, Tabitha Brown, and Ashleigh Shanti are among the top Black women chefs. They have made significant contributions to the **culinary world** through their appearances on television cooking shows and through their cookbooks. Each has a unique approach to cooking and has inspired many with their culinary skills.

Black Women Athletes!

Simone Biles, Serena Williams, Naomi Osaka, Allyson Felix, Venus Williams, Simone Manuel, Gabby Thomas, Jordan Chiles, and Crystal Dunn are some of the Black women athletes who have shattered barriers and set new standards in their respective **sports**, including gymnastics, tennis, track and field, swimming, and soccer.

Black Women Holistic Health Practitioners!

Dr. Carmen James, Aala Marra, Dr. Ruby Lathon, Marisa Hall, Joycelyn Elders, and Alexa Canady are among the most notable Black women holistic health practitioners. They have dedicated their careers to promoting holistic health, advocating for **preventive care**, and integrating traditional **healing** practices with modern medicine.

Black Women Herbalists!

Henrietta Jeffries, Emma Dupree, and Brianna Cherniak have preserved and advanced the knowledge of herbal medicine, providing **natural remedies** and promoting the healing power of plants.

Black Women Yogis!

Maya Breuer, Krishna Kaur Khalsa, and Michelle Cassandra Johnson are pioneers in bringing yoga and **mindfulness** to diverse communities. They have been instrumental in highlighting the importance of inclusivity in wellness spaces.

Black Women Scientists!

Katherine Johnson and Gladys West have made ground breaking contributions in mathematics and computing, laying critical groundwork for space exploration and GPS **technology**.

Black Women Poets!

Phyllis Wheatley, Maya Angelou, Sonia Sanchez, Jessie Redmon Fauset, Frances Ellen Watkins, and Aja Monet have captured the essence of the Black experience through their **poetry**, advocating for justice, love, and equality.

Black Women Inventors!

Shirley Jackson (Fiber-Optic Cables), Marie Van Brittan Brown (home video security system), Lyda D. Newman (hairbrush), and Patricia E. Bath (Laserphaco Probe) have contributed significantly to **technological advancements**, improving daily life and medical treatments.

Black Women Psychologists!

Inez Beverly Prosser, Beverly Daniel Tatum, Jennifer Eberhardt, and Mamie Phipps Clark have contributed significantly to our understanding of racial identity, educational psychology, and the impacts of racism through their **research and clinical work.**

Black Women Engineers!

Annie Easley, Dr. Donna Auguste, and Mae Jemison's noteworthy accomplishments have significantly impacted the fields of **engineering** and technology and paved the way for future generations of women in STEM.

Black Women Authors!

Toni Morrison, Audre Lorde, Gwendolyn Brooks, and Bell Hooks have profoundly impacted **literature**, offering critical insights into race, gender, and societal issues through their work.

Black Women Pastors!

Jarena Lee, Julia Foote, Pauli Murray, Bishop Yvette A. Flunder, and Rev. Raquel S. Lettsome are trailblazers in religious leadership. They have opened doors and fostered inclusive **spiritual** communities.

Black Women Accountants!

Mary T. Washington Wylie, CPA, Kendra Dancy, CPA, Gerri Lazarre, **CPA**, and Charisa Price, CPA, are pioneers in the accounting field. They have broken barriers and established a legacy of excellence and leadership.

Black Women Lawyers!

Constance Baker Motley, Michelle Obama, Kamala Harris, and Loretta Lynch have been at the forefront of **legal advocacy** and public service. They have championed civil rights and broken new ground in their professions.

About The Author

Phyllis Y. Whitley is a remarkable individual who has dedicated her life to helping others. She is the CEO and founder of Self Whisper, LLC, and WhisperVise, Inc., a non-profit organization. Phyllis holds a Bachelor of Science degree in Psychology and Religion Studies and a Master of Arts degree in Human Service/Wellness from Liberty University. She is a certified Holistic Health Coach.

Phyllis has been a go-to relationship guru since her teens and is passionate about helping women overcome relationship drama. Her journey has led her to discover that God desires to bless us holistically so we can do His work in the marketplace while living in our promised land. She has overcome many challenges in her life, including cancer and religious bondage, and now uses her experiences to guide others into a voice of victory.

Phyllis is an Ordained Minister and a Prophetess and uses her education, skills, and experiences to empower and deliver people from religious bondage and relationship abuse. She is a sought-after holistic relationship consultant, prophetic teacher, visionary writer, mystic podcaster, and motivational speaker who keeps it real and raw for her clients. She teaches and builds prophetic prayer warriors and Christ-conscious leaders by example.

Phyllis represents herself using a sweet-smelling rose born from her broken whispers, a meaningful symbol throughout her brands.

She now resides in the Midwest with her family. If you are looking for someone to help you overcome relationship drama, religious bondage, or any other challenges in your life, Phyllis Y. Whitley is the person to turn to.

Self Whisper, LLC. www.SelfWhisper.com
WhisperVise Inc. www.WhisperVise.org
Podcast: Spiritology Live (on multiple platforms)
Youtube: @selfwhispervise

"Beloved, I pray that you may prosper in all things and be in health, just as your soul prospers."

3 John 1:2 (NKJV)

PHYLLIS Y. WHITLEY BOOK COLLECTION

DISCOVER THE POWER OF HER BOOKS DEDICATED TO HEALING YOUR MIND, BODY, AND SOUL!

WORDOLOGY

* SPIRITOLOGY

*ASK JALEN!

*#1 Amazon Best Sellers

WHISPER-ME WISDOM JOURNAL

SELF-WHISPER MEDITATION THERAPY & DEVOTIONAL POETRY

PROPHETIC WHISPER BOOT CAMP (PWBC)

WHISPER-ME JOURNAL FOR PODCASTER

WHISPER ME GOD'S COLORS

WHISPER ME GOD'S COLORS II

WHISPER-ME JOURNAL FOR WOMEN

For as he thinks in his heart, so is he.
Proverbs 23:7 (NKJV)